Contrails

and Other Life Tracks

Stafford W. Edwards

Published by Cynaptic Press, 2022.

Contrails and Other Life Tracks

Copyright © 2022, Stafford W. Edwards

Cataloguing data available from Library and Archives Canada

Web Site: https://library-archives.canada.ca

ISBN: 978-1-7387374-1-3

E-book ISBN: 978-1-7387374-0-6

(E-book available for Kindle, KOBO and Apple iBooks)

Contact information: Email: author@cynaptic.ca
PO BOX 99900 LU 893 596 Ottawa RPO Strandherd
Ottawa ON K2J 6B5

Dedication

This book is dedicated in loving memory of my son Isaac, whose name means "Laughter." There will come a day of Laughter when our family will be made whole again.

Table of Contents

Preflight

Preparation. That thing you do before attempting a task, especially one which is unfamiliar or daunting. Some tasks are quite routine yet require great vigilance. Pilots do this before, during, and after every flight. Similar elements can and should be applied to our lives as well.

This book is not about navigating the upper atmosphere, though it does engage the use of aviation metaphors for descriptive resonance. It is also not a list of do's and don'ts on being successful, nor is it meant to be another how-to manual. Instead, my sincere hope is for this manuscript to provide a useable level of clarity for anyone travelling along life's pathways. Consider it a personal source of encouragement from me to you, the reader.

This will primarily be anecdotal in nature—a few exposés and vignettes from my life, each containing key elements which have impacted me since childhood. I have experienced many significant moments through the various intersections my life track has crossed. They have not only been instrumental in shaping my character but have also contributed to the ongoing evolution of my personality, which in turn has revealed strengths and vulnerabilities through the choices I have made. All of which make a case for discovering who I am as a person.

Acquiring invaluable life skills usually comes through the process of learning how to adapt to life's unpredictability. Throughout our lives, we are presented with opportunities, though not always in a manner we desire or expect—or even recognize. Some may even consider that these life-impacting thresholds arise at the most inconvenient of times. The thing is, even with careful planning, living one day at a time, and with measured consideration, you will never be completely prepared for every contingency. That, however, should not be a reason to throw out hard-won strengths or lessons you have acquired throughout the journey. This revelation also brings another vital aspect of our humanity to light, one which is often overlooked due to its seemingly ethereal construct— the vibrancy and validity of dreams.

At first glance, dreams may seem intangible and devoid of any practical value. We often dismiss them as being inconsequential. If, however, we were to consider dreams as encompassing cherished aspirations, ambitions, or ideals, they can help instigate purpose. Purpose begets a plan; a plan allows for the implementation of action, and action has the ability to take us into opportunity. Interestingly, opportunity may also embody purpose, which can lay the foundation for destiny—even for a young child.

Perspectives about life tend to ebb and flow as we mature. As we progress from childhood into adolescence, adolescence into adulthood, and then move into the silver- lined years, the ideological lens of youth loses some of its focus and conceit. While this isn't a forgone conclusion for everyone, I do believe it holds traction for most people. For myself, at times throughout my life, it has proven a challenge to accommodate a balanced, hopeful attitude, especially when buffeted by unwelcome and unexpected events.

But what happens when you discover that the very processes ostensibly designed to enable you to live a full and abundant life, are not so structured or do not form the paths you envisioned for your life trajectory? We then need to consider this; no one treatise can provide non-interruptible success and balanced stewardship for your life.

The challenge then is to acquire actionable intel to rectify this seeming life imbalance. I do not have a catch-all solution, as I am but one man after all. What I can share, however, is perspective. Over the years, I have gleaned from others with similar experiences and, just as importantly, I have learned from my own successes and failures. It has taken quite some time for me to understand and appreciate the intimate relationship between success and failure. They are essentially two sides of the same coin. One is not necessarily better than the other, at least as far as gaining a clear understanding of who we are is concerned. We should also be aware of how we see ourselves in contrast to how (we think) we are perceived by others. Not understanding this duality can add an unhealthy tension to our already overstressed lives.

Our perceptions and experiences in life are influenced through such filters as the emotional, physical, financial, spiritual, and cultural, to name a few. Having a healthy appreciation of your true identity and intrinsic value is of vital importance, not only for yourself, but for any who happen to be in your sphere of influence. No matter your age or status in life, the journey of learning about yourself never really comes to an end. With all of this in mind, allow me to share a few of the more indelible, life-defining scenarios I have wrestled with. Some have been conquered, while others are still in a state of flux as my life journey continues. All quite normal, as I endeavour to wear the skin of humanity in as healthy, productive, and purposeful a manner as possible.

> *So, I concluded there is nothing better than to be happy and enjoy ourselves as long as we can. And people should eat and drink and enjoy the fruits of their labor, for these are gifts from God (Ecclesiastes 3:12-13, NLT).*

Ignition Sequence

What ignites your passion? What area of your life becomes fully alive as you think, work, play, or converse? What easily captivates your attention or distracts you from other pursuits?

Consider the things in your life which capture your imagination. For myself, I am convinced I fell in love with aircraft at the moment of conception. Well, I may be romanticizing my earliest memories of an ongoing passion just a little, but according to family lore, I was conceived during a time when my mother was employed in the Air Traffic Control system in Jamaica. Now, I have no way of determining if the vocation of one's progenitors actually determines your dream quotient, but as far back as I can remember, I have always been enamoured with all things related to aviation.

In retrospect, the thoughts and stories contained herein can be traced back to a mutual decision made by two individuals, who sixty years ago pledged themselves to each other in marriage. Approximately two years after this momentous occasion, I came into being. Little did my parents know at the time their decision would initiate an indeterminate number of ripple effects reverberating through a timeline spanning multiple decades.

As a child, I was fortunate to have parents who consistently encouraged me to work hard and give my best in every task I put my hands to. However, I did not always agree with their work ethic. In fact, there were times I demonstrated outright stubbornness and apathy. The tendency to let things slide was always close to the surface. Even closer to the surface was the occasional application of painful—yet justly deserved—parental discipline whenever I strayed across the ever-decreasing line of insolence and misbehaviour. During those formative years, growing up with corporal punishment did not have the restrictions (some would say stigma) of political correctness as it does in this day and age. Others may disagree, but because of the loving discipline of my parents, I gained intimate knowledge of the consequence of error, along with the sustaining practice and benefit of wisdom.

The earliest recollection of my passion for aviation came the first time I was afforded the opportunity of flight. My parents informed my brother and me, then seven and ten years old respectively, we would be departing from Kingston, Jamaica by plane and flying to New York City to visit relatives. Up to this point in time, I had only admired these gravity-defying marvels from a distance, either in flight overhead or seen parked on the airport ramp. When the day came, I could barely restrain my excitement as we shuffled along the slow-moving queue leading to the ticket agent. I remember my parents calling me back several times, telling me to wait for my turn.

To a ten-year-old, a McDonnell Douglas DC-8 aircraft may as well be the size of Canada. Wheels, wings, engines, everything about the plane captivated me as I drew closer. If left to my own devices, I would have initiated my own preflight inspection, but a ten-year-old's musculature is not sufficiently developed to wrest control from acutely attentive and deceptively strong mothers. Finally reaching the bottom of the air stairs and staring up an incline reminiscent of an Aztec temple, I proceeded upwards with renewed enthusiasm.

Cresting the top, we were met by what I firmly believed was an angel from heaven. To say I was immediately smitten with the flight attendant would be an understatement. Oh, I had seen them in passing inside the airport terminal, but in this case, I was the focus of her undivided attention—at least until the next person behind me followed. As I was ushered aboard, I caught a glimpse of the cockpit, and tunnel vision immediately locked into place. Although I was too young to appreciate the complexity of what I saw before me, there was an immediate resonance which surpassed my original encounter with the celestial being who had just greeted me. Knowing this was where the aircraft was controlled from, I then made it my goal to learn all I could about what it would take to fly an aircraft.

A non-stop commercial flight from Kingston's Norman Manley International Airport (MKJP) to New York's John F. Kennedy International Airport (KJFK) is approximately three-and-a-half hours. It took two minutes to be seated and strapped in, fifteen minutes to complete passenger boarding, and ten minutes to taxi to the active runway before experiencing what can only be described as *The Rush*! Having never before experienced a take-off, the event crystallized another defining moment in my decision to pursue my dream of flying aircraft. What would cause some to grip their armrests with white-knuckled tension, provided for me an excuse to release even more endorphins—entities I had no idea existed in me at the time.

Contrary to popular and misguided belief, measurable testosterone levels do exist in ten-year-old boys. Although likely to be in a somewhat dormant state, they should never be dismissed out of hand. The evolution of sound in concert with the increase of jet engine thrust, defied gravity's hold on the aircraft, immediately pushed me back into my seat, shoved me past pre-adolescence, and catapulted me headfirst into post-puberty, all in the span of time it took the aircraft to complete its take-off run and depart the runway. Watching the ground drop away as we gained altitude provided me with a unique and captivating experience—one which would become a pivotal part of who I was destined to be.

My inaugural flight also allowed me to unconsciously disprove certain scientific and anthropological theories. One being only those of Afro-Centric origin are equipped with broad, flat noses. I would like to propose that the application of constant pressure of one's nose against tempered plexiglass at 35,000 feet, for over three hours, may also promote the same physiological disposition, regardless of your melanin quotient.

The equally fascinating flight regime of approach and landing, allowed for fidgeting on an order of magnitude which may have caused my parents concern, had it not been for the convenient restraint of my seat belt. My window seat provided an unrestricted view of the left wing, and from initial descent to final approach I bore witness to the hydra-mechanical metamorphosis involved in transitioning a hundred-ton aircraft, flying at just under the speed of sound, to one skimming along at one hundred and fifty knots just prior to touchdown. The wing, a sleek, smooth, inanimate appendage while at cruise altitude, now suffered from an identity crisis. It sprouted flaps, panels, screw-jacks, hinges, and servos, all working in concert to provide high lift at low speed. Not realizing the best was yet to come, at the moment of touchdown and just prior to the crescendo of reverse thrusters and g-force induced braking, the wing seemed to literally come apart. It fulfilled its final role of the flight by killing all lift as quickly as possible when the spoilers automatically deployed as the main wheels touched the ground.

This experience was irrevocably imprinted on my psyche, and it took place a few months prior to my entrance into high school. With this dream of flight now seeded and about to germinate, one would think I would be fully committed to the required discipline and scholastic engagement necessary to become a pilot. The problem was my next life threshold involved being introduced, quite unexpectedly, to a couple I would come to know as the Twins of Disaffection. They were Isolation and Puberty.

Train up a child in the way he should go, and when he is old he will not depart from it (Proverbs 22:6, NKJV).

Transition Altitude

The Twins and I entered high school just prior to my eleventh birthday. My age at this point may seem confusing to some, and no, I was not a child savant, or even remotely genius level. In fact, I was pretty average. I began my high school adventure at a decidedly British all-boys boarding school nestled in the hills of central Jamaica in the parish of Manchester. Outside of England's borders, you could not find a more tropical, British-infused environment. Back then, Jamaican children started high school earlier than those in North America, following the British educational curriculum of that era.

Now some may say uprooting a young eleven-year-old boy from his family and familiar surroundings, then transporting him to live in (what seemed to me at the time) a pseudo-prison for young boys for the purposes of education was a bit harsh. Well, I suppose that thinking is understandable. I do recall suffering deep anguish as I watched my parents drive away after dropping me off on my first day. Having never before experienced the weight of separation from family, an acute sense of loneliness descended on me. I experienced this each time I returned from a school holiday or started a new school year.

One argument advocates the nurturing and training of a child be accomplished within the family nucleus, where emotional support, coupled with balanced discipline and love, are administered. Not at a cold institution with a formidable, prison-like regimen. The opposing position argues for the forging of independence and self-reliance as early in life as possible. The child would learn to devolve their dependence on parental security and begin to learn what it means to fend for themself. This second scenario comes with a few elemental risks.

One not only has to weigh any cultural factors, but also the child's maturity and emotional levels—elements which begin development early in life but are not fully established until well into young adulthood. However, in our efforts to discover what constitutes balanced or healthy support outside of the immediate family, we should also be aware that not all family units provide the best opportunities or atmosphere for the proper development of young children. While those formative years in boarding school were foundational, and in some cases intrinsically good for the development of who I am today, it goes without saying not all my experiences were enjoyable, or beneficial.

This boarding school was a beast unto itself. In the past, I often wondered who established this particular institution in the central rolling hills of this tropical island. A child my age would not be privy to the real motivation behind this, nor would they have an understanding of the variables associated with being educated in an all-male environment such as this. Certainly not the sort of thing a young child thinks about, because not more than half a mile down the road was the sister school to the one I attended—a decidedly non-British, all-girls boarding school. Introducing an eleven-year-old boy into the potentially charged social environment these two institutions generated, would normally require proper guidance and counsel, preferably from mature mentors with hard-won experience. As it turned out, I was surrounded by other eleven to sixteen-year-old boys, who themselves could not deduce the difference between wisdom and a wicker basket. Part of the problem was this school's administration being more interested in scholastic aspects of development than social or nurturing ones. I have a better understanding now of what I stumbled through then.

The transition from child to teenager is fraught with many potential pitfalls. As I mentioned earlier, one of the original uninvited vagrants, Puberty, ingratiated itself during this dangerously delicate period of my life. With the emotive equivalent of a Category 5 Hurricane, it struck without warning. Since I had never been around so many older boys at the same time, I had never been exposed to, well...things older boys have to contend with. Maybe never having an older brother left me ill-equipped to understand the subtle, and in many cases, overt interplay between young male teenagers and those of the opposite sex.

An all-boys boarding school in the hinterland of a small tropical island may not have been the most socially advantageous location to transition from child to teenager. Having no grid or reference by which to measure how I should comport myself, I was left with limited choices. One, I could imitate what I saw the other boys doing, or two, I could somehow figure out how best to remove or insulate myself from the unfamiliar influences surrounding me. Given this boarding school was, for all intents and purposes, a swirling, hormonally charged, teenage Gulag, my escape options were severely limited. This revelation then gave rise to a new commodity. Fear.

Fear, as it turned out, was the second cousin of the aforementioned Twins and promptly joined them in being the driving force already clouding my destabilized emotional state. Even at eleven years of age, one can easily identify frontal systems of fear, rejection, and pain. Someone just has to look at you with derision or indicate intent to harm. This in turn can be the catalyst for emotional or even physiological distress, which can lead you into the arms of Isolation. You know very quickly what it feels like to not be part of the in-crowd. This was a common theme for me while attending this school, and it fed the acute sense of dislocation I felt being away from my parents. I had been thrust into a new environment, replete with older, testosterone-infused, alien bipeds from other mothers, who seemed to sense in me the very fear I was having a hard time coming to terms with. Adding to the intense emotional upheaval I was experiencing, I soon found myself in what I fully believed was a fight for my life.

This unfortunate privilege came to me through the unpleasant process of hazing. At first, I did not identify it as such, as eleven-year-olds normally do not have a reference grid with which to prepare for such a thing. What I quickly discovered was I had no real choice in the matter. You see, the initiation process at this particular school was quite severe. Most assuredly for one so young. This involved being given a choice. For every new student boarder attending this school, the senior boys forced them to either submit to fighting with them or choose another new student to fight instead. This was a full-on, fist-foot-teeth, anything goes kind of get-to-know-you introduction. So, I did what any oppressed, backed-into-a-corner constituent would do; I exercised my right to vote for the lesser of two evils. I chose to fight a new student—someone with whom I hoped I was on equal footing in strength, or at least of a smaller stature than myself.

The outcome turned out to be a resounding success. For the other student that is. He managed to demonstrate with efficient alacrity, and in no uncertain terms, how tenacity can trump size. Not to mention experience. I found out later he was a bona-fide scrapper, long before he ever attended this school. My consolation prize after this ordeal was a painful and tearful two or more hours on my bunk bed, wondering how I managed to take a wrong turn into hell. It was at this point in time my emotional scars started a courtship with the new physical ones I had just received.

There are many who have suffered levels of pain deeper than I have. They have come under abuse too heinous and painful to come to grips with—at least on their own strength without any kind of external support. Whether you are young or old, we all are susceptible to wounding. Most physical wounds can heal. The unseen ones can take much longer and, in some unfortunate cases, never fully heal. Some of these hurts may have been given to you as a child. These wounds can stay dormant for years and become resurrected, even when exposed to influences or outside forces not related to the initial cause of your wounding. It goes without saying; if you are unaware of what is affecting you internally, it becomes all the more challenging to recognize there is a problem. This is especially true if it has been entrenched for a long time.

Therein lies a key. What you are exposed to at an early age can have an exponentially enhancing or debilitating effect on your future disposition as an adult. As adults, we cannot go back in time and redo our childhood. Sometimes hindsight can be a gift; to others, it can feel like a curse. Regardless of which camp you find yourself in, there is still the opportunity of gleaning insight from those experiences. There are times when we are unwilling to derive meaning from experiences which may have caused disappointment or pain, especially if it requires revisiting the very thing which caused distress in the first place. We are not naturally predisposed to moving towards things that make us uncomfortable—no matter how good it will be for us in the long run. Rectifying issues of this nature requires an honest acknowledgement and acceptance of their existence. Any past or current wounds need not define who you are as you learn to move forward in your search for healing.

When I was a child, I spoke as a child, I understood as a child, I thought as a child; but when I became a man, I put away childish things (1 Corinthians 13:11, NKJV).

Departure Clearance

Acquiring direction and focus for your life can be attained through various forms—mentorship, self-discipline, vocational study, or even spiritual pilgrimages. These are just a few sources which allow for focused vision to be established. In addition, giving yourself permission to be yourself also allows for the opportunity to dream and take risks. Yes, even if those endeavours potentially lead to failure.

Prior to entering Aircraft Maintenance Engineering in college and, later on, Commercial Flight Training at university, I attended three high schools spanning two countries. The first being the private boarding school I mentioned earlier, and the second, a public day school in Kingston, Jamaica. I also attended one other public high school for Grade 12 when I first moved to Canada. If I add up my accomplishments from the three schools, I would rate my scholastic achievements above average.

I was still carrying six years' worth of accumulated teenage introspection when my family emigrated to Canada, just one month prior to my seventeenth birthday. After one year in a new country, with a new and vastly different educational curriculum, I found myself on the threshold of entering my first post-secondary institution. One obstacle however, narrowed my path forward significantly—my GPA. It was not sufficiently robust to allow entry into college.

At the age of eighteen, the unresolved residual effects of Fear and Isolation still lurked within me. By this time, these entities had silently morphed into a low-grade form of self-loathing. I became my own worst critic. If I was not successful at something I had tried once, twice, or even three times, then for each perceived failure or regression, I convinced myself I was no good. The proverbial fuel on the fire increased when I was left to repeat a semester to improve my grades after my friends had successfully graduated from high school the first time around.

The thing is, prior to having my dream of flight fulfilled, I had to learn stuff. A lot of seriously important and necessary stuff. The kind which forces you to recognize that if you are going to work on, or fly aircraft, you need to have an intimate understanding of principal forces you cannot take for granted—such as gravity and all of its idiosyncrasies. Let's not forget other mandatory requirements like aerodynamic lift and drag coefficients. You know, the sort of things geared to make an untrained brain hurt. Unknown to me at the time, I was about to be on the receiving end of one of the most insidious sneak attacks ever to cross my then young life. To an adolescent with big dreams, it was the mother of all ironies.

The ambush came in two parts, as ironies are known to do. The assault was very tactical and split into two segments, which then executed a flawless pincer move, cutting off any real or perceived option for retreat on my part. The first part initially seemed harmless, which essentially agreed with this premise; I was irrevocably besotted with aircraft and anything related to them since my first testosterone-revealing flight as a child. The second part mercilessly began a campaign of mockery against the very thing I had fallen in love with.

Before the development, training, and completion of my passion could be realized, I had to confront a childhood nemesis—Math. This basically boiled down to: I did not like it, and it did not like me. Needless to say, the conundrum of loving something passionately, but loathing the necessary requirements to accommodate the fulfilment of said passion, provided for a good number of years of tortured introspection.

I was never one to be classified as an A-student. At least not as far as Science and Math went. I had to work doubly hard to attain a GPA that granted me access to higher levels of education related to my vocational dream. My initial college program of choice after graduating from high school was Aircraft Maintenance Engineering. One inviolable truth of successfully pursuing your passion is it usually requires effort, dedication, sacrifice, and an unquenchable desire to succeed. You will, however, face opposition from various quarters. It may be from those known, or unknown to you. More often the obstructions come from within oneself. As things turned out, I had to retake several exams in order to complete the Engineering program. Adding insult to injury, after finally making the grade to successfully graduate from college, failure was threatening an encore.

In order to pass the program's next level and acquire my Engineering license, I had to take a number of federal government exams within a set timeframe. There were five exams, and after taking the first one, I was unsuccessful. I wrote the second one and failed it as well. I rewrote the first one after the required waiting period and failed again. To be honest, I cannot recall if I actually attempted to rewrite the second exam, but I do know I entered a depressive state. I was in an emotionally precarious place, enough to cause my parents to be concerned. During that dark period, I recall my father asking me what I wanted to do with my life. Initially I was unsure, but as time progressed, I began to understand he was actually enabling me to contrast where I had been and where I was then, with where I hoped to be in the future. It took me a fair amount of time to reconcile I still had a future. My passion had not died; it was only overshadowed by doubt and confusion.

Our emotional state at any given time can either illuminate, deflect, or filter out altogether the light of hope. I was fortunate to have parents who saw my potential and loved me enough to hold me accountable during those times of distress. This allowed me to prepare for an unexpected turn of events, all within a few weeks of the failures I had just experienced. I was going to start Commercial Flight training at a new university.

To say lingering doubts were in abundance would be an understatement. My efforts at reconciling the exam failures immediately after college were still on shaky ground. Instead of learning how to fix aircraft, I was now getting ready to learn how to fly them. I would have to negotiate the mental balancing act of actually launching a contraption made up of thousands of pounds of metal, rubber, and aviation gasoline in a questionable attempt to defy gravity for an allotted period of time and return to Earth safely. I would also be required to digest aeronautical and meteorological rules and regulations, grasp the theory of flight, acquire and manipulate the new language of air traffic control, and make enough sense of it so as not to cause undue calamity to myself and others. Initially, this was accomplished with a flight instructor—one with nerves of steel and the patience of Job.

After graduating from college, I spent two years at university training to be a Commercial Pilot. As it turns out, I was good enough to receive an award for being one of the top student pilots in my first year. While this gave me much needed motivation and confidence, it was in the final stages of my flight training when my emotional fortitude was tested once again. The important yet daunting final exam, necessary to become certified as a fully licensed Instrument-rated Commercial Pilot loomed before me. Despite many hours of study—both in theory and actual flight time—the Instrument Flight test truly intimidated me. Successful completion would allow me to operate an aircraft using the onboard instruments to follow a given route of flight, with no need for visual reference to the ground.

The exam lasted approximately three hours. In the final eight minutes, just as I was cleared by Air Traffic Control onto the final approach to the active runway, the Federal Flight Inspector sitting beside me and grading my flight informed me I had just failed the flight test.

Once we landed and parked the aircraft, we had a detailed debrief. The very first thing the Flight Inspector said to me was he had just witnessed one of the best instrument flights he had ever seen during his career as a flight examiner; right up until those final minutes when I failed to comply with a vital instruction from Air Traffic Control. It turned out I had inadvertently descended below a final assigned altitude given to me by the Approach Controller. My lack of attention to this mandatory instruction was instant grounds for failing the exam. My abject sense of failure in that moment brought back painful memories. I was afforded the opportunity to retake the exam a week later, but, while I was proficient enough the second time around to pass the flight test, given the associated tension from the earlier failure, it was not completed with the same level of precision as my initial attempt.

Looking back at the turmoil I experienced then, what remains is not the bitter pill of failure, but this realization—even in the midst of what seemed a crisis of confidence, a simple acknowledgement of what was done right in the moment, provided a redeeming element of hope. I was told I had executed a flawless flight up to a point where I momentarily lost focus. Because the Flight Inspector first highlighted what was positive with my flight performance, I was able to receive and manage the negative impact of the hard lesson regarding my altitude-busting mistake. It also allowed me to understand my dream was not crushed, just bruised.

You do not have to know how to fly a plane to appreciate there are some things which should be attended to with care and acute attention to detail. If you find yourself coming up short in those areas, and invariably we do at times, it does not mean all is lost. We all have in us the capacity for accomplishing great things, even when the inherent processes involve failure. Failure, however, can be a vital ingredient for providing a firm foundation from which we can build towards the fulfilment of our hopes and dreams.

The steps of a man are established by the Lord, when he delights in his way; though he fall, he shall not be cast headlong, for the Lord upholds his hand (Psalm 37:2324, ESV).

Turbulence

Roses have a sweet aroma and are beautiful to gaze upon. They also have thorns, which cause pain if they are not handled carefully. When pressures in life assail us, we at times lose sight of our innate value. Invariably, we never consider that which causes us pain may be the very thing which not only strengthens us, but also allows us to bloom right where we find ourselves.

Turbulence is never a comfortable feeling. It not only has the capacity to make you nervous, it also heightens your sense of not being in control. Whether you experience turbulence while flying, being beaten up as a young child in boarding school, or attempting to navigate emotional turmoil as an adult, it can undermine any semblance of peace and contentment. Turbulence has also been known to invite its partners in crime, Stress and Tension, to come out and play.

Some time ago, while considering this uncomfortable state, I began thinking about the comparative natures of how engines operate in contrast to how we operate as individuals. From a mechanical point of view, the essence can be summed up in four decidedly inarticulate words: *Suck-Squeeze-Bang-Blow.*

"

These descriptors summarize the principles of engine combustion: *Intake-Compression-Ignition-Exhaust*. They also help define a few lubricating components necessary in the forging of our character as we progress through life; things like *Submission-Pressure-Discipline-Activation*.

I believe the elements of physics represented within the laws of nature were divinely set in place for our benefit. I would go further and say physical and spiritual laws can be interchangeable-to the point of being connected to one another. Just as today's modern combustion engine would be considered witchcraft to those in the first century BC, the principles for being emotionally and spiritually balanced may seem rather antithetical in the scope of our modern, fast-paced, humanistic society. Taking all of this into consideration, let us break a few things down.

Intake. Breathe In. Submit. Think about breathing for a moment. You normally have limited choice in the matter. In fact, you are automatically configured to inhale. We do it whether asleep or awake, without conscious thought. But suppose you choose not to inhale? Initially, you have control over your breathing. Before long, you will be compelled to take a breath. Some who have a stronger lung capacity may even go for a long time without inhaling, maybe even beyond the point of consciousness. But as soon as that happens, the body kickstarts itself into breathing again, without any voluntary input from you. Submission in its purest form is like breathing. It's automatic and without conscious thought. When we consciously choose to stop breathing, there may be a span of time where things seem to be in control, but eventually there is an inevitable consequence of action. Just like the physical law—*for every action there is an equal and opposite reaction*—a spiritual law demands a response to anything which either acts in concert with it, or against it. Submission is a catalyst, an accelerant. An engine needs the intake of air to be mixed with fuel in order to begin the process towards propulsion.

Then there is *Compression. Being Squeezed. Under Pressure.* We do not lend ourselves well to things causing discomfort. Personally, I am allergic to all forms of pain. I tend to break out with symptoms of whining, complaining, anxiety, and other such illness-inducing dispositions. You know the breath you took before? The one that for the most part was involuntary? It needed to be compressed and mixed. You breathed in, and oxygen was forced into the alveoli in your lungs. The alveoli are the final branching of the respiratory tree and act as the primary gas exchange units of the lung. This compression mixing process serves a dual purpose. Clean oxygen inbound; poisonous carbon dioxide outbound. All done through the same interface. Okay, if you have stayed with me thus far, it gets better, although it may feel worse.

You have allowed yourself to breathe naturally; to submit. You feel by doing so, things should be running along smoothly. The problem is your propulsion seems to have stalled before it even started. You are not even moving! You have submitted. You have inhaled clean air, with the full intent of exchanging it for the bad. You believe you have completed all the right steps, drawn the necessary logical conclusions to getting something done. Maybe a wrong needing to be made right. Or a fresh start at a new job. Or possibly a renewed commitment to a spouse. As you ponder all of this, you start to smell smoke.

Ignition. Discipline. So, things are starting to heat up. When last did you identify, or even take a look at your *Comfort Zone*? We all have one. Actually, we usually have more than just one. Your comfort zones are areas in which little or no voluntary movement takes place in any direction, usually resulting in unexpected dissociative behaviour. Contrast that with *Zones of Contention*: areas which usually require a lot of movement. A zone of this type tends to involve heat, pressure, pain, and an involuntary tendency to question the reason of all things, including your existence.

During the time of America's engagement in the Vietnam War, there was a frightening weapon of mass destruction employed. The weapon was called Napalm. It consisted of Naphthenic and Palmitic acids—a thickening, gelling agent, usually mixed with gasoline or a similar fuel for use in military operations. When used as a part of an incendiary weapon, napalm causes severe burns (ranging from superficial to sub-dermal) to the skin and body, along with asphyxiation, unconsciousness, and death. Its explosions can create an atmosphere of greater than twenty percent carbon monoxide and firestorms with self-perpetuating windstorms of up to seventy miles per hour (110 km/h). One of the main features of napalm is that it sticks well to exposed skin and hence leaves no real chance for removal from the skin of the victim.

Now, I don't know about you, but at first glance, this whole idea of breathing in the first place seems, well, a tad risky? By now, it's easily understood that breathing/compression/mixing is necessary. Why are we now throwing incendiary components into the mix? There is a principle at play here. Movement is impossible without ignition. Mixing air and fuel while adding heat results in a combustive reaction which has to go somewhere. The maximum take-off weight of a Boeing 747-800 series jet is 975,000 lb (442,000 kg) or approximately one hundred and six full grown bull elephants. For an aircraft with that amount of weight to even move on the ground, it requires four engines, all generating sustained, controlled explosions in sync, giving a combined generated force of approximately 180,000 pounds of thrust.

Discipline rarely feels gentle, or even comforting. Discipline, if understood correctly, is not punishment. Punishment implies the infliction of a penalty as retribution for an offence. Discipline, on the other hand, is the practice of training an individual or group of people to abide by rules or a code of behaviour. Yes, some (in fact most of society) would call that punishment, but punishment does not carry the true essence of discipline. Discipline can (and should) include demonstrations of love, dedication, or commitment. Whether from a loving parent who administers discipline to train a child, or you as an individual attempting to train your body for running a marathon or studying for an exam.

So, alveoli exchange good air for bad, just as a combustion chamber combines an intense fuel/air mixture in order to provide motive power. Discipline generates in us the capacity to move, to not remain stagnant. It's freakishly painful at times. It's meant to stick permanently— like napalm. There is an interesting side note to the aforementioned principles. What at first feels oppressive allows one to not only move, but move in a direction that tends to contradict the effects of the applied forces at play. Just as the immense weight of the 747 jet starts to move against gravity, you are now moving forward in direct opposition to what you are facing or *feeling, or* by what was holding you back.

This now brings us to *Exhaust. Propulsion. Thrust. Activation.* A jet engine's intake air flows opposite to the direction of flight. Exhaust (thrust) moves a multi-ton aircraft and launches it into the air against the natural forces of gravity. This continual process of *Intake-Compression-Ignition-Exhaust* allows for this. The interruption of just one element in the flight regime will result in catastrophe. Therefore, *Submission-Pressure-Discipline-Activation* generates the momentum to move against that which opposes us. Like putting your mind and body through the extensive training process required to prepare yourself mentally and physically to become a soldier. The removal of any one element in the process can yield unpleasant consequences.

One important thing to remember, whenever you find yourself in the turbulent combustion cycle of life, wherever at all possible, be aware of your breathing. Most often it's an involuntary, subconscious thing, but there are other times we may be required to control *how* we breathe.

Therefore we will not fear, though the earth give way and the mountains fall into the heart of the sea (Psalm 46:2, NIV).

Flight Plan

The space between your conception and taking your final breath encapsulates your life journey. What transpires while travelling along the route between these two points, quantifies and qualifies your growth as an individual. We face the volatility of a future, one which is not always in line with our expectations.

24 hours earlier...

Excitement started to build once I found out I would be introduced to cross-border flight procedures. My university flight instructor was going to take a couple of his students from Langley, British Columbia into Washington State to teach not only advanced flight navigation, but the differences between US & Canadian flight and ground operations. The main intent was to acquire the skills and knowledge necessary to safely traverse from Canadian to US airspace, land there, and then, return, hopefully without initiating a cross-border war.

We had flown many times into US airspace but never before had we landed an aircraft on US soil. We always flew back into Canadian airspace to our home base airport. These particular airspace segments in question, overlapped Southern British Columbia and the northern sectors of Washington State. To make things even more interesting, shortly after entering US airspace, depending on your direction of flight, not only would you speak with civilian Air Traffic Controllers, you were also required to contact US Navy Military Controllers in charge of restricted military airspace along the Western Washington coastline.

And so we began to prepare for the upcoming flight. This was back in the days when passports were optional, so a federally issued Canadian Commercial Pilot's licence sufficed. Preparing for any flight requires a significant attention to detail. Planning a flight into what is effectively a foreign country, even more so. You had to let them know you were coming a minimum twenty-four to forty-eight hours in advance, in what type of aircraft, along with a complete passenger manifest. All aircraft airworthiness logs and, of course, your pilot's licence had to be up to date. On top of that, you had to compile a flight plan detailing your proposed route, and that was dictated by a thorough review and dissemination of meteorological data along your intended route of flight. After all that, you had to file your flight plan in advance in order to get it into the Air Traffic Control system. Then, on the actual day of the flight, you are required to complete a full pre-flight inspection of your aircraft, checking for leaks, anomalies, or other things that could physically impede or affect your aircraft, on the ground or in flight.

The day finally arrived when all pre-flight forms, transmissions, checks, and the weather cooperated to actually allow me to fling myself skyward. We ventured south into the

US and hopped throughout the San Juan islands, into airports with exotic names such as Anacortes, Samish, Guemes, Sandovi, and Fidalgo—names that sounded more at home in Puerto Rico than the State of Washington. We then looped back into Canada via Victoria, to clear Canadian customs before heading back to our home base in Langley in the Lower Mainland.

24 hours later...

With the previous day's flight still fresh in my mind, I was required to complete the same flight solo as part of my training. I was permitted one passenger who was not a pilot, so I asked one of my friends and she agreed to go along for the day's adventure. With flight prep out of the way and round-trip flight plan already filed, I once again headed south.

Things started to get interesting after being handed off to Washington's Air Route Controllers. My initial visual flight-planned altitude was for five thousand five hundred feet, but given the penchant for unpleasant weather to rapidly form on the west coast, I was forced to request a lower altitude below a three-thousand-foot cloud deck I swore was not there a minute before I made contact with Air Traffic Control. Our first destination was Bellingham International Airport. We were vectored toward the airport and, once given clearance, we landed and taxied to the area where itinerant pilots park to clear customs.

Because of the requirement to file a flight plan and set up customs notification ahead of time, a US Customs Agent will normally be aware of any foreign private aircraft arriving at a

US airport. With that in mind, I parked in the designated spot, not expecting a long wait. After fifteen minutes we started to get antsy. Thirty-five minutes after putting the parking brakes on, worry began to set in. When fifty minutes ticked over, I decided to venture forth from the aircraft to the Customs building approximately one hundred metres from the plane.

I had not taken two steps toward the Customs building when an agent emerged and started walking towards my plane. Nervously, I watched him stride toward me with grim intent—a huge holstered firearm fastened to his right hip and a look of pure disgust and indignation written on his face. As he came up to me, any preconceived notions of me owning personal space were totally obliterated!

To say this guy was angry would be the ultimate understatement—and, initially, somewhat puzzling. He wasted no time in getting right up in my face and proceeded with a dressing down that would make a Marine drill sergeant proud. After excavating and then demolishing any vestige of well-being I had remaining, he asked to see my flight documents as well as my passenger's. Unfortunately, I also made the mistake of forgetting to ensure that my passenger's birthdate was filled in the proper place on the form. This then provided another opportunity for the agent to initiate another salvo at my shredded demeanour.

Here is the deal. Back then, pilots of arriving private aircraft were required to remain in the aircraft. The Customs Agent comes out to meet them. Given that I had landed an hour earlier and had not been met by anyone, I assumed that Customs had not received notification of my arrival, for whatever reason. Now for the real kicker. This was the same

Customs Agent who had cleared my aircraft not less than twenty-four hours earlier, along with my flight instructor, myself, and two other students. He most certainly knew who I was, and he was well aware of the fact I was a student in training. Needless to say, his countenance was polar opposite from that of the previous day.

I was twenty-four years old when this incident transpired and I was on the cusp of another uninvited, unexpected life lesson. It did not take long for me to ascertain this particular Customs Agent had an issue with anyone with a naturally deep tan being allowed to operate an aircraft, much less having the audacity of landing it in his backyard. It would not be the last time I encountered such a scenario. There were times before and after when I am sure I missed the cues, but for the most part, I tend to give people the benefit of the doubt. But, at times, you are taken completely off guard.

Racism, with its inclination to denigrate those caught in its crosshairs, has been a poison through many generations and across many cultures. Whether overt or subtle, it corrupts the instigator and wounds the recipient. It can be extremely difficult to maintain your composure if you are the victim of this kind of onslaught. I have been denied jobs because of that mindset, as well as overlooked for promotions, only to find out too late after the fact as to why.

Where do you draw the line? How do you protect yourself? How should you deal with this type of antagonism? This is where having a clear understanding of your true identity comes into play. Your perception depends on several factors, including, but not limited to, your upbringing, your culture, your education, even your emotional and spiritual equilibrium.

Possessing an astute awareness of your inner self not only mitigates arrows of ignorance being shot in your direction, it also affords you the ability to deflect or nullify their impact through the extension of forgiveness. Forgiveness is a powerful weapon against ignorance. You do not forgive to excuse the wrong being inflicted upon you as a person. Rather, you give it to release *yourself* from the insidious potential of sliding down the dangerous slope towards your own bitterness and hardness of heart. Extending forgiveness is more for you than the person who may not even deserve it.

If I am being honest, I can say with certainty I was not in a forgiving mood after being put through such an emotional wringer by this Customs Agent. I still had several stops to make throughout Washington State before safely returning my passenger to Canadian airspace, so I had to get my head in gear for the remaining portion of my flight. When we finally landed at Victoria International Airport on Vancouver Island to clear Canadian customs, and after having been so effectively chastened earlier, I was determined to stay put, no matter how long the Agent took. As I taxied up to my designated parking spot, I noticed someone leaning out of the terminal building's doorway leading to the Customs area. He was waving at me to come inside.

I am now thinking, "Fool me once" ...but he persisted and, so, after completing my shutdown procedures, both my friend and I exited the aircraft, fully expecting to be shot on sight. When we did get inside and produced our documents, we got a Customs Agent with not so much as a pea shooter in sight!

Customs Agent: "Howzit goin' eh?"

Me: "Fine," I lied.

Customs Agent: "Been hoppin' the islands again?"

Me: "Yes, sir."

Customs Agent: "Anything to declare?"

Me: (Thinking: Yes...there be crazy people south of the border!) "Ahh...no sir."

Customs Agent: "Alrighty then...have yer'selves a safe flight back to the mainland!"

Oh, how I love Canada!

But I tell you, love your enemies and pray for those who persecute you (Matthew 5:44, NIV).

Gravity

Defining and refining your inner strength in spite of your circumstances can provide clarity to the natural expression of who you are. This may include identifying and wrestling with the very source of fear, confusion, or perceived weakness you experience. Even with your destination in sight, sudden microbursts of contention may arise to throw you off track. Intentionally facing the obstacles which threaten your progress, however, can bolster your maturity and inner strength.

There are times in life when we feel we are continually buffeted by headwinds. Naturally, it would be so much easier to have the relief of a tailwind now and again. I was thinking about this one day when I received a text message from a friend. It read, "They say one has to first jump before your parachute is able to open. I get that. But in your search for purpose in life, what do you do when you don't know what it is you want to do?"

It was quite an insightful question. I did not immediately respond but thought about it some more, and given the context of the query, I wondered if you should jump anyway, even before acquiring a definitive answer. A primary goal of jumping with a parachute is to ensure the chute opens from a predetermined, safe altitude. Where you land is just as important as how you land. If your initial landing point is unknown prior to (or even after) jumping, your plan of action for an appropriate conclusion is always the same—a safe, controlled landing.

You need to continually assess your surroundings, along with wind direction and speed, rate of descent, etc., to make sure you have acquired all proper information before reaching your touchdown point. All this to determine how best to prepare for whatever terrain is rising up to meet you.

There is another important thing to note, but one less easily or readily embraced. The fact is, while you are descending, you have the opportunity to take in the view from your current—albeit rapidly changing vantage point. Maybe the revelation or realization of where your landing zone is located requires information gathered during the (sometimes uncertain and, yes, risky) journey toward it. Other times, you may be presented with vistas (opportunities or scenarios) which are only accessible at elevations above your intended point of arrival.

So, if you lack a purpose or goal in life, perhaps you first need to develop the courage to jump in the first place. In short, you need to take a leap of faith. When attempting to exercise any level of faith in something, or someone for that matter, there is this undercurrent of dynamic tension. You are taking a risk with something that seems counter to what you are used to or comfortable with. In light of this, I have always wondered about the dichotomy of opposites, or more definitively, things that oppose or seem to contradict. For example, why do we park our cars in a driveway and drive on a parkway? Why is sour milk considered bad and sour cream good (according to some)? Why do feet smell and noses run? Why do we ship by truck and send cargo by ship? How can a SLIM CHANCE and a FAT CHANCE be the same, while a WISE MAN and a WISE GUY are opposites?

If there are extra-terrestrial beings out in the cosmos being inundated with Earth's firehose of radio and television transmissions, I believe we have no reason to fear a planetary invasion. Any species capable of intergalactic space travel surveying us from afar, would either be dumbstruck with confusion or be totally out of breath (assuming they breathe a gaseous mixture) from laughing too hard—or whatever passes for laughter for them.

It has been said that there is good and bad cholesterol, and good and bad stress. Are opposites required to be either bad or good? Not necessarily. You can have opposing viewpoints on a matter that do not make one individual right over another, just different. Some would argue this point of view does not necessarily hold true for some of life's more acute challenges, especially those which may be truly oppressive on many fronts—whether physical, emotional, verbal, or otherwise. Or how about meeting the challenge of aspiring to something that you have never accomplished before? What would it take to stay the course, even if the chosen path contains blind corners, which in turn conceal drop-offs that may not give you any advanced warning?

I received unexpected inspiration after reading about a certain aviator—Felix Baumgartner. On October 14, 2012, halfway to outer space, he stepped out of his high-altitude capsule, which was tethered to a balloon, and plummeted back to Earth from more than 120,000 feet (twenty-four miles) above Roswell, New Mexico. The forty-three-year-old pilot became the first person to break the sound barrier outside an aircraft, reaching a Mach speed of 1.24 (834mph/1343km/h). To break the record, he literally stepped off a tiny ledge outside his capsule, a pod-like unit that carried him nearly twenty-five miles up into the stratosphere by a super thin, fifty-five-storey-tall balloon that Red Bull and he designed for this skydive from space.

I can only imagine the seemingly insurmountable challenges that Felix faced as he prepared for this endeavour. The aspect that fascinated me most, however, was the actual moment when he physically left the capsule. For several hours, he was strapped inside a tiny, certainly claustrophobic area, as it transported him up to the edge of space. Then, when the moment arrived for him to exit the capsule, the door slid open and he was faced with...space. A lot of it; and he did not hesitate.

Talk about opposites. Try to imagine going from a secure (albeit small) enclosure to the vastness of space; from claustrophobia to the potential for agoraphobia. Obviously, Felix does not suffer from that malady. He knew the risks, yet, when the time came, he stepped out into thin air. In addition to the physical act of leaving the capsule, he was also mentally ready to leave that definitive yet temporary comfort zone.

Unfortunately, many of us miss out on life because of instinctive fear. The point being that, if you wish to live your life to the fullest, you cannot do so without some element of risk. Therein lies another opposite; risk-taking goes directly against our human desire for self-preservation. I also learned another fascinating lesson from watching Felix's record-breaking feat. He used to his advantage the same force which opposed him all the way up to the time of his jump. The very thing that sought to prevent his success allowed him to succeed. He used gravity to set a record. Now that's going with the flow!

So, we can settle for a life that is safe and boring, or choose one in which we bravely face the inevitable pressures of the opposites and be rewarded with new vistas along the way. We so often fail to realize that in order to get the best view, we have to climb to a higher elevation - whether by stairs, a mountain, or in a balloon to the edge of space. The ability to endure these and other types of stresses, can strengthen who we are as individuals. It does require effort - at times for lengthy periods, other times less so. But be assured; the rewards for our efforts are more than worth it.

For God has not given us a spirit of fear, but of power and of love and of a sound mind (2 Timothy 1:7, NKJV).

Contrails

Consider the tracks your life generates. How do you view them? How are they perceived by others? What are the life lessons and legacies which follow in the wake of your life's journey?

At the risk of sounding immodest, I consider myself a level-headed individual and not prone to irrational displays—at least not the sort that would cause those around me to recoil in shock. I am also allergic to pain— emotional, physical, psychosomatic—it doesn't matter. I personally believe most, if not all people, have an aversion to pain on some level. I am yet to meet a person who is immune to its influence. Depending on the severity and the type, one could break out in fits of pouting, whining, stubbornness, confusion, grief, anger, and yes, even tears.

I also like to cook. Well, I tell myself that thing I do to prepare a meal actually passes for cooking. Some time ago, I was gathering ingredients for a dish I had made many times before—successfully, I might add. The lead-up to all of this involved running around dealing with unrelated errands.

Now, I am what some may describe as a contemplator. I tend to ruminate and cogitate. Basically, I think...a lot! I would consider a thing from every possible angle in order to come to a conclusion. At times, finding the correct answer to some of my challenged thought processes, are elusive at best, non-existent at worst. What generally ends up happening—according to those around me, is I seem to take too long to come to a decision on any given subject at hand. While the wheels are turning in my head, it does not come as any surprise that I may miss things now and again.

This particular case in point had to do with getting home from the grocery store with the aforementioned ingredients. I was planning to prepare a meal for my wife, who was returning home from out of town. I placed the grocery bags on the kitchen counter and began preparations. Vegetables were taken out and washed, sliced, and then put aside. Next, the meat was unpackaged, cut up, and seasoned. The stove was turned on and olive oil was measured into a saucepan that was then placed on one of the stove's elements. Turning back to attend to other side dishes which I proudly assumed would splendidly complement my culinary masterpiece, I was struck by a thought (go figure). The thought translated into a subliminal undercurrent of fear and then paused just below the threshold of panic. It occurred to me, while I was merrily shopping for groceries, I had taken my iPad with me. After taking a quick look around, any contemplative tendencies instantly evaporated as I realized I had not come back home with it. In fact, coming into view in my mind was the exact location where I had left it. In a shopping basket I had placed on the floor while waiting in the cashier's check-out line.

With this mental imprint providing more than enough motivation, I immediately grabbed the car keys and made haste back to the grocery store. Upon arriving, I went directly to the same check-out line I had used earlier to see if per chance the iPad was still there. Not a tablet in sight. Then, approaching the lady by the cash register, I asked with mounting trepidation if anyone had seen or turned in an iPad. She said she did not think so, but then she called the office and, joy of joys, it had been turned in. So, after retrieving it and clutching it like some mother with a returned lost child, I retraced my steps home, which was only a two to three minute drive away. After parking the car and walking up to the front door, I started to hear whistling in my ears. Initially I ignored it, not paying much attention, but the closer I drew to the front door, the whistling transformed into a high frequency pitch.

Do you recall that previous undercurrent of fear? The one that stopped short of the threshold of panic? Well, not only did it refuse to wait anymore, it promptly changed clothes and proceeded to break all previous land speed records in getting to the *Panic Zone.* Contrary to popular opinion, time does not slow down when one faces adrenaline-inducing stimuli; it comes to a complete standstill. Opening the front door, I was met with the full onslaught of sound, smell, and no sight. The sound was from the fire alarm going off, and just in case I missed that subtle cue, it was also screaming at me in French and English, informing me there was a fire taking place. The smell was that of acrid smoke, generated from one of nature's tastier fossil fuels—olive oil. The lack of sight was due to white, billowing smoke throughout the house and somewhere inside, amidst the cacophony of noise, our white and now totally camouflaged dog was cowering while trying to figure out how she ended up in Hades.

Jumping ahead ten minutes, after all the windows and doors were opened and fans were set to full blast, the walls and rest of the house came into view—along with the dog. As I viewed the results of my involuntary attempt at scorched earth theory, I found myself moving closer to another threshold of panic—how to convince the soon arriving wife I had not been playing with a flamethrower in the kitchen. With melted cabinet doors above the blackened stove and adjacent walls, as well as soot throughout the main and upper floors, especially on the ceilings, I briefly entertained the panicked (and yes, completely idiotic) notion of blaming the dog. Fortunately, she is too cute to get mad at. And so began six weeks of insurance estimates, removing everything, I mean everything, from the house, along with dealing with work and life in general.

We put ourselves at a disadvantage if we give in to the feeling that life only consists of burdensome things. This unfortunate event was inconvenient, yes, but we were extremely grateful no one was hurt, and we did not lose our home. At times, we are going to have challenges which test us, but never underestimate your value as a person—even when you make errors in judgement. For the longest time, I loathed making mistakes, especially when my intentions were to do the right thing. Sometimes, the only way to learn or grow is through the uncomfortable process of trying and failing, oftentimes repeatedly.

By going through these processes, we may discover the measure of our character is directly proportional to the crucible of our life's narrative. This was a lesson which has taken me years to understand and accept. If I am being honest, there are still elements of this truth I am learning to come to terms with.

Remember, the process of learning who you are as a person is ongoing, and is not only discovered through mistakes, but through triumphs as well. There are times when we do get things right, even during the most unexpected of circumstances.

One such scenario transpired over seventeen years ago. It happened on one of those occasions when I was driving with my eldest daughter, who was sixteen at the time. Out of the blue, she asked me a question:

"So, Dad, at what age should I start dating boys?"

Although spoken in a regular conversational tone, those words seemed to explode against my auditory receptors. I somehow managed not to swerve off the road. The fact I am here telling this story is not so much a testament to my driving skills, but has more to do with what I truly believe is God's Grace. It brought into sharp relief two things that impacted me viscerally. One: how best to answer this question in a manner that encourages and edifies my daughter. Two: I was stunned (but genuinely happy) she was comfortable enough to pose the question to me in the first place. I cannot remember exactly what my response was to her query, but I do recall it was done with carefully chosen words of encouragement.

Now move ahead eight years. I found myself sitting in the living room of the condominium where my daughter and her husband of six months now reside. The juxtaposition of my daughter's sixteen-year-old query contrasted with me sitting in her new home, years later, is both jarring and serene. The same can be said for my two younger children. As young adults, they too are still being transported through life with deep questions of their own. Some have been answered; others are yet to be.

As a father, I am acutely aware of my deep-seated desire to be able to provide any and everything necessary for the well-being of my children. Yes, even as adults. A significant portion of that responsibility has been transferred to my eldest daughter's husband. It's now his mandate to be her covering in all aspects. I still love and pray for her, but my daughter's life-stream baton, which I had been carrying since her birth, has now been transferred to my son-in-law.

An admittedly unsettling fact, for me at least, is I will never be perfectly successful at being a parent. This then begs the question; what is the true litmus test of successful parenting? Yes, it's unrealistic to expect perfection of yourself (or others for that matter), but human nature being what it is, we tend to wrestle with things which evoke conflicting emotions. I have since come to realize, it's not so much a matter of being perfect, but being consistent in my efforts, when endeavouring to operate with an attitude of excellence. If you fail, and you will, then try again. Oh, one other thing; learning to forgive yourself is also a challenging but necessary requirement when you fall short of any real or imagined level of expectation you have burdened yourself with.

As you get older, there is an inevitable increase in frequency of mulling over your life's accomplishments—or lack thereof. You also start thinking about what you will leave behind. I have learned legacies are not as tangible as we sometimes make them out to be. While I may not have a trust fund of Bill Gates' proportions to bequeath to my children, I desire to see them successful in all their endeavours. Yes, materially, even though material wealth is not a requirement for a balanced and well-adjusted lifestyle, but more importantly, socially, emotionally, and spiritually, among others.

Our family has suffered through loss as much as we have experienced joy. Those tangible intangibles will be with all of us until our final breath. Looking back on what has transpired over my life thus far, while looking forward to what is yet to be, provides an opportunity for me to gain perspective on my purpose(s) in life. Some are easily defined—work, pay bills, put food on the table. Others, while not as definitively mundane, I believe carry more weight. Showing compassion to others; teaching others through your life experiences; understanding sacrifice; loving unconditionally; allowing your children to express themselves or pose questions without fear of judgement, just to name a few. In essence, acquiring and having an appreciation for a purpose-filled life.

Consider the tracks your life generates. How do you view them? Do you know how they are perceived by others? What are the life lessons and legacies which follow in the wake of your life's journey? We may be oblivious to some of them; others are more readily identifiable. However, they can and do have a lasting impact on any who come under our sphere of influence, by the intersecting of their own life paths with ours—even if just for a short time.

I have discovered one aspect of who I am, though, and that is having an appreciation for the correlation of who I love and who I am loved by. This then gives me confidence in gaining a better understanding of who I am yet to become.

I praise you because I am fearfully and wonderfully made; your works are wonderful, I know that full well (Psalm 139:14, NIV).

Explosive Decompression

It has been said that time heals all wounds. I would propose time "tempers" wounds instead. The acuteness of the pain may diminish with time, but there is a rule of investment we need to be aware of. The depth of love you carried for the person you lost will determine the depth you will grieve for them.

April 29th, 1998

I woke up at 4:00 a.m. to prepare for my 6:00 a.m. shift at work. Outside was shaping up to be another standard day with an expected high temperature of 15° C. While the rest of my family slept, I showered, got dressed, and followed my usual morning departure ritual which consisted of lightly kissing my sleeping wife and then looking in on my children: my two girls—Rebekah, ten years old and Naomi, seven years old; and my two sons—Ethan, five years old and Isaac, nineteen months old. The previous night I had the pleasure of cuddling and playing with Isaac in my bedroom. After he had fallen asleep in my arms, I carried him to the room he shared with his brother and placed him in his crib.

On that morning, after first checking on my girls, I crossed the hallway to my boys' room. As I peered inside, I noticed the pre-dawn tinge of light on the sky's horizon filtering through their bedroom window, promising another pleasant Spring day. I quietly stepped towards Ethan and gently touched his head. I then turned and approached Isaac's crib and did the same. It struck me then just how contented I felt in that moment. As I reflect on that time, I feel somewhat conflicted. Possibly because I have struggled so often since then, when trying to capture the same feeling of contentment. Interestingly, that very struggle may in turn hold the solution. Somehow, my contentment seemed easier to come by back then—with little to no effort.

I went downstairs, grabbed my jacket and the car keys, went outside, and locked the front door. The drive to work would take fifty minutes. Traffic was light at that time of the day and the morning commute always provided opportunity for my thoughts to roam freely. On this particular morning, I was thinking of a special project I was involved with at the Air Traffic Control Centre where I worked. I had been involved with this project for a couple of weeks and found it quite stimulating. I was looking forward to getting another productive day completed.

Four hours after arriving at the airport, I was deep into my work when I got the call. It was from a close family friend. She said Isaac had an accident in our home and had just been taken by ambulance to our local hospital and I was to leave immediately. I asked what had happened, but she kept insisting I come right away. Needless to say, I departed immediately. As I drove out of the parking lot, a million thoughts ran through my mind. I do know I started to pray. Not knowing what had transpired, I began asking God for protection and health over my son. I also found myself making declarations out loud as I drove to the hospital— statements such as:

"Okay, God, what's going on? What are you saying to me right now? Whatever is wrong with my son, please remove it from him. Transfer it to me, if that is what it takes!"

I made it to the hospital in a significantly compressed timeframe. I parked and ran into the emergency room where I was met by another friend. He happened to be the Children's Pastor at our local church, and he knew our family well. It turns out he had been waiting for me to arrive, and before I could even get a word out, he said,

"I am so sorry, Stafford. Isaac did not make it."

He said it so softly I thought I misunderstood, but the drawn look on his face was more than enough to confirm my worst nightmare coming true. It was then I heard the anguished wailing coming from a room behind him. I knew immediately who it was, even though I had never before heard such sounds come out of my wife. The sound and the pain behind it prompted an automatic shunt to be put in place for my own shock and confusion, at least temporarily. In that time span, what mattered most to me was seeing what I could do to alleviate the pain my wife was suffering. The rational part of me knew there was little, if anything, I could do to bring relief for her. But the protector in me was wired to try, regardless.

As I entered the room where my wife was waiting with a few other friends, I still did not know what had transpired. I cannot recall if it was my wife or one of our friends who ultimately informed me about what had happened. Isaac had been playing around an open reclining chair when it accidentally closed on him. As I held my wife, my earlier temporary emotional shunt began to crumble.

September 23rd, 2022

Today, I am now someone who I was not in the past. Suffering loss has a way of jolting you out of a zone of oblivious comfort, while at the same time assaulting you on deep emotional levels. It's not a voluntary initiative. It's never something we choose. In fact, it's diametrically opposed to our human nature. In times past, I would never have given deep thought to mortality—mine or anyone else's. We don't naturally lend ourselves to cataloguing the extent of our remaining days. It does go without saying, if we find ourselves facing a potentially terminal ailment, there is a significant increase in the clarity of how we view our life. However, this also happens when you are not the one facing a life-limiting condition.

It is now 2022, and it has been twenty-four years since we lost our son. This year, on September 23rd, he would have been twenty-six years old. More than old enough to have legally acquired his driver's licence or cast his vote in elections. Graduation from college or university would likely have already been completed. He may have had a girlfriend, or even been married. We find ourselves grieving for a daughter-in-law whom we will never meet. He would have had ample opportunity to laugh or cry, be sad or happy, or be angry or confused.

These are normal emotions we all have, long before turning the age of twenty-six. Mourning the loss of a loved one does not just entail everything prior to their passing. We mourn their (and our) lost futures as well. What could have been. What should have been.

I am not who I was twenty-four years ago. Twenty-four years ago, a knife went through this family's collective heart, unbidden and without warning. The initial process of grieving was unfamiliar, decidedly alien. It felt not of this world. But grief is so interwoven with this fabric called life, there are times when it causes us to question our reality, while bringing into focus the very mortality we vainly try to ignore.

The pain borne out of the loss of a loved one can be so intense that it debilitates us. While it has been said that time heals all wounds, I would propose time "tempers" wounds instead. The acuteness of the pain may diminish with time, but there is a rule of investment we need to be aware of. The depth of love you carried for the person who passed away will determine the depth of grief you will experience. In short, you are forever changed. You cannot go back to the way it was before. If you could, then the wound would be fully healed. So, because we cannot go back in time to change the outcome, time will never fully complete the healing process.

On the surface, this may sound less than encouraging. In time, with loving care and support, it's possible to move forward in spite of the pain. Living a full, productive, hope-filled life, even with a heart scarred by loss, is attainable. Often it feels as if we could never experience such a life again because of the deep pain we find ourselves in. It's okay to feel that way. Your loss is unique to you. Even if others have lost loved ones, they do not have complete knowledge of how you feel about your loss. They may have a sense of connection to your pain because of the unfortunate bond of loss you both have in common, but we each process our grief uniquely.

So, what is there to be done, if anything, about this burden we did not ask for? Well, there is at least one thing—we can learn to reconcile the loss. It does not mean you deny your pain. In fact, reconciliation not only acknowledges your pain, it also provides an avenue for healing the now changed person you are. Dreaming, laughing, and hoping again is possible in time, but again, only as the changed person you are now, not the old you before the loss. Reconciliation allows us to continue the process of mourning our loss, even if we cannot attain the answers as to the why, or even how something so traumatizing transpired. As much as we would like to achieve a satisfactory conclusion to what is a very tiring process, you are allowed to process grief at your own pace. There is no set time limit.

Some time ago, my cousin's son-in-law passed away from cancer. He is survived by his wife and two daughters, the youngest of which was born only a few days after her father died. My cousin is in pain for his daughter's loss, just as he is in pain for himself. How does one reconcile the joy of a new birth and the sorrow of your daughter losing her husband in the span of one week? I believe that takes no small amount of prayer, and time. As long as is necessary. There is no set limit on reconciliation. Additionally, those grieving should never have to do so on their own. For us, faith, family, and friends become our lifeline.

While working on this very chapter of the book, I wept bitterly as I took time to remember my son Isaac. I chose to engage in grief work. Yes, grieving is hard work, but necessary. It allows your mind, soul, and body to continually adjust to your new normal. It's not a normal I would have chosen, but it happens to be my reality now.

Twenty-four years of ongoing reconciliation have transpired. Have levels of healing taken place? Yes, in many ways, but at times I still feel pain, some very intense even after all this time. The pain you may be feeling now is normal. Whether you have just lost a loved one, or if it has been many years, you are free to grieve in your own way.

So, how do you recognize when you are processing your grief in a healthy manner? Well, there is one guideline we can follow. So long as you are not causing any direct harm to yourself, or to someone else, physically or otherwise, whatever expression of grief you choose then is normal and okay. Some cry, some scream from the top of their lungs, some get angry with God, while some have to engage in something physical like gardening or chopping wood. Some grieve without any outward sign of emotion. Also, be aware, as your journey of grief unfolds; do not be surprised if you find yourself behaving or thinking in a fashion which seems contrary to how you functioned prior to your loss. You may find some things now seem to have a higher priority than they did before your loss, like taking time for yourself, or others. You may even find that a once annoying trait in a friend or loved one may seem less so. Remember, you have been impacted on deep levels. You will need time to adjust.

As you interact with those suffering through loss, please be mindful of this; you cannot curate or catalogue their process of grief and mourning. The pain of the loss of a loved one does not end, but the intensity of the pain can alleviate over time. The person in whom you invested your love has left a hole in your heart—a hole which outlines their shape, their memories, their life, their legacy. Do not let anyone try to tell you to get over that.

> *Beloved brothers and sisters, we want you to be quite certain about the truth concerning those who have passed away, so that you won't be overwhelmed with grief like many others who have no hope (1 Thessalonians 4:13, TPT).*

Hypoxia

"I know I don't look it, but I'm beginning to feel it in my heart. I feel thin; sort of stretched like butter scraped over too much bread. I need a holiday, a very long holiday..." (Bilbo Baggins—The Lord of The Rings/The Fellowship of The Ring by J.R.R. Tolkien)

After a rough night of fitful sleep, you awaken and look outside the bedroom window with bleary, sleep deprived eyes and gaze upon sun-drenched autumn foliage, colourfully contrasted against a bright blue sky. A part of you (reluctantly) acknowledges nature's wardrobe change, but there is a sense that change has been underway in you as well. It just now happens to be coming into stark relief as you ponder what has transpired over the past year to this moment.

One of the hardest things a man may struggle with is how best to bring his mind into submission, arresting errant thoughts and soul-leeching notions of how things seem versus how things really are about himself and others. That is the crux of the matter. What you see and perceive compared to what is reality and truth. You would think the two positions would be mutually exclusive. Things can get downright fuzzy when the mind is left to its own devices.

When he interacts with those around him, he occasionally glimpses irritation, impatience, and, in rare moments, disdain in their eyes. Interestingly, he does not hold that against them, as he too has directed the very same emotions toward himself. After all, have there not been many opportunities and sufficient time to get one's act together? This, of course, cycles right back into his filtered perception of things versus the truth of what is real. Much has been taught and written throughout history about what it takes to become a man—aspects of living out a life that fills him with challenge, hope, destiny, and purpose.

Where does a man find the inner fortitude to persevere when challenges become crushing weights? When hope turns into despair and destiny looks like a shimmering far-off mirage, how does one reconcile having a purpose for existing? Some men embrace extreme sports to challenge themselves physically and mentally. Some volunteer in the military where similar challenges are thrust upon them. Others attempt to scale the corporate ladder, while others find satisfaction in creating large or intricate structures with their hands.

Invariably, these types of men have inborn talents that allow for the expression of the aforementioned endeavours; but what about those men who are not classified as Type A specimens? Are they exempt from the visceral thrill of testing their mettle, or living an exciting life on the edge? Not every man is expected to be a SEAL Team Commando, but no less important is the fact that *all* men deserve to be fulfilled in life—even when life seems unfulfilling. As I wrestled with these thoughts, I recalled a question which asked, "If you had access to a time machine, would your first trip be to the future or to the past, and why?"

It took about ten seconds for me to decide that my first trip would be to the past. Mainly to observe, but with an added caution. We are frequently encouraged to "always look to the future." There are, however, critical and invaluable lessons to be learned from things that have already transpired. Any foundation on which we now stand (political, socio-economic, cultural, scientific, religious, familial, along with many others) has its philosophy rooted in that which has preceded us. Wisdom is the acquisition and application of knowledge gained through the pressures of experiencing life. With that understanding, one caveat becomes evident; there is a primordial risk in having clear and unfiltered access to the past via a time machine. We may be tempted to prevent our younger selves from going through the same pitfalls, and in doing so, we would effectively eradicate everything we have learned from these mistakes in the years to follow. While circumventing any historical unpleasantness of the past is something many would no doubt choose, there are just some things that can only be learned by experiencing them, as difficult as those situations may be.

If we had prior knowledge of potentially unpleasant experiences and were offered the opportunity to sidestep them to avoid emotional, physical, or otherwise debilitating trauma, we likely would do so without a second thought. That would be natural, as our natures are averse to all forms of pain. Yes, it's daunting, frightening even. Some might disagree, but given the historical "nature" of human nature, things easily acquired without resistance or investment of time, energy, and sacrifice, usually result in the devaluation of not only the process, but the very things being sought.

Let's say someone gives you a car, versus you working hard for many months to save enough money to purchase one. There is added weight in value brought to something you have worked hard to attain, because you're intimately aware of the effort that was expended to acquire it. Your appreciation of its value will lead you to take better care of it.

Should this argument apply to all situations related to unfortunate times of pain or loss? No. I would never advocate for every form of crisis, pain, or trauma for the benefit of acquiring life lessons. That would be at a minimum counterproductive and callous in the extreme. At this point in my life journey, where matters of the heart and mind are concerned, I can only speak for myself, not others. If I could go back in time, I would do everything in my power to circumvent the loss of our youngest son. It's highly probable I would not care about garnering any latent "life lessons" or substantive wisdom through having my life irrevocably turned inside out through such an ordeal. What still remains as truth, regardless of my feelings, is this: Knowledge plus Experience still equals Wisdom. Because I follow a faith-based tenet which ascribes to a Creator who is loving and just and has my best interests at heart, I find myself in an extremely uncomfortable position when posed a frightening (at least to me) question. Would I trade any divinely appointed Wisdom gained throughout my life in order to receive my son back? I am no giant of faith as Abraham was depicted in biblical Hebrew and Greek writings, and my son, Isaac, who carries the name of Abraham's son, was never required or intended to be a sacrifice, but sacrifice nonetheless has transpired. I am learning that at times, when personal yet troubling questions are posed, whether by ourselves or others, they may fall into three categories:

- *Questions without immediate or readily identifiable answers*

- *Questions that are not the right ones being asked*

- *Questions just needing to be asked, irrespective of the preceding two conditions*

Either of these three elements can allow for the foundation of reconciliation—a difficult, and, at times, exhausting process, but one that allows for the ability to address, or at a minimum, consider difficult or unanswerable queries about life. One thing is certain, no amount of questions or lack of answers will ever erase the love we have for our son Isaac.

I have come that they may have life, and that they may have it more abundantly (John 10:10, NKJV).

Holding Patterns

An aircraft in flight is slowed down by headwinds if it does not counter with increased thrust. However, increasing thrust increases fuel consumption and shortens the range of the flight. This is where careful pre-planning comes into play prior to departure. For us, this can be a foundation from which we can build our own reserves when facing obstacles.

Monday

The start of the traditional work week. I awoke this morning telling myself it was going to be a good day.

My body was not in total agreement, but it had no say in the matter. Little did I know that it also turned out to be a perfect day for a blood sacrifice. I involuntarily attempted to offer up portions of the Elixir of Life via a measuring cup.

I headed downstairs to the laundry room to gather clean clothing and, in the midst of said mundane activity, I knocked over a glass measuring cup on a shelf I brushed by. Isn't it wonderful how time seems to slow down and speed up all at the same time, as your retinas process the millisecond snapshot of the (now) unavoidable consequence of error? The sudden deceleration forces imposed upon said glass container, coupled with feet and toes conveniently positioned within the rapidly expanding blast radius of silica shrapnel, made for an unsurprising stroll down the avenue of self-recrimination.

Embracing déjà vu, not less than forty-eight hours before, whilst engaged in another mind-numbing activity (cleaning the floor), another object fell because of my clumsiness. Klutz. Jinxed. Accident Prone. Butterfingers. As I berated myself, I realized there is a course of action we may take during such inconvenient circumstances.

We have choice.

We can choose how we respond to unexpected, sometimes painful stimuli. A healthy, thoughtful response usually depends on the immediate condition of our hearts, and/or disposition of our minds at the moment of greatest vulnerability. Sadly, I admit I do not always present an attitude of forbearance under such situations. But just as flossing your teeth regularly aids in the prevention of tooth decay, undergoing various levels of character-building moments (physical, spiritual, and otherwise) provides opportunities for growth and maturity, which go a long way, preparing us not only for life's inevitable challenges but also for the rewards, both now and those yet to be realized.

I do not wish to portray life as consisting only of repeating problems. When we try our best, but fail at accomplishing something, those moments of disconnected feelings may cause us to question the sufficiency of the very efforts we expend. Any subsequent dissatisfaction could be formed by an overly high expectation of oneself. Maybe something which, in your opinion, should have already come to pass in a reasonable amount of time. Unfortunately, we can be our own worst critic at times. Conversely, our disillusionment could be a result of our perception of someone else's behaviour or reaction towards us.

I have learned (still in process actually) that unhealthy defence mechanisms are usually deployed to protect our feelings from pain. For example, if I decide to degrade myself before someone else has a chance to do it to me, I have made an assumption out of fear. My (incorrect) thinking is that I have depleted the power or sting of any argument they might have before they have a chance to use it against me. If they proceed to critique me anyway, I convince myself that by pre-emptively putting myself down first, I have diffused any presumed leverage or criticism they have over me.

We each have our own way of dealing with the challenges life throws at us. Some methods are healthy, some are not. But realize that even when life seems to be going well, there will still be moments when we may feel insignificant or inadequate—when we feel devoid of any meaningful purpose. Normal life involves having the wind occasionally leave our sails. I am not advocating we remain or become stagnant in our emotional doldrums, but sometimes we have to wait on the wind to pick up before the sails can snap back into place to get us moving again.

Something else to bear in mind while you are waiting—it's a good time to check what is stored below decks. Lighten the load. Consider throwing overboard anything not needed. Just remember to keep the sails unfurled, as you do not want to miss the returning wind. You just never know when or from which direction it will begin to blow again.

> *The wind blows wherever it pleases. You hear its sound, but you cannot tell where it comes from or where it is going. So, it is with everyone born of the Spirit* (John 3:8, NIV).

There are times when I still question my thoughts and wrestle with preconceived notions. I recall one particular time of struggle, as it happened under grey overcast skies. Trees were laid bare due to cold driving winds carrying flecks of snow and ice pellets which stung the skin on contact. Dry, dead leaves were blowing randomly about, signalling the onset of the unwelcome seasonal transition to a Canadian winter.

Whether you are suffering from the winter blues or experiencing cabin fever, atmospheric seasonal changes not only affect, but, at times, can reflect the soul. Personally, my favourite season is summer. Warm sunshine, no need for layers of clothing, everything is green, fresh, and alive. Did I mention about it being warm? One good thing about winter though—you always have something to look forward to—spring's new growth; the inevitable banishment of the cold; the warmth of new beginnings. Spring is always guaranteed to follow.

It turns out these positive thoughts were in the foreground of my mind, two weeks after having been let go from what I considered to be the most satisfying job I have ever held. For fifteen months, the routine of getting up early and commuting to work felt, well...just right. That feeling may have had something to do with the fact that, prior to this past position, I had been out of full-time employment for almost two years. The struggle was real, and it took some time and effort not to succumb to self-recrimination and self-doubt. After wrestling with the ghosts of past job losses, I was finally able to defeat any residual hold over my bruised thought processes. I set out to acquire and maintain an attitude which allowed for the expectancy of bigger and better things to come.

I do not want to make light of the circumstances surrounding the loss of a job. I have swallowed that bitter pill several times in my life. In fact, thinking back over the intervening years since graduating from university, I have changed jobs six times. Of those six transitions, three have been involuntary. I can at least take (small) comfort that being let go had everything to do with the companies' bottom line rather than a fault on my part—or so I was told.

With all this in mind, we can once again remind ourselves of that one universal truth—change is constant. Weathering the storms of life can be distressing at times, but these challenges may also hold unexpected value, just as distressed leather is immediately recognized by its unique patina, one resulting from rough use and agitation. At first glance it seems battered and worn, yet it is soft, supple, and durable. Because of these characteristics, it's readily sought after and prized. Could it be the seemingly repetitive trials we face throughout life are opportunities to showcase our own yet to be recognized patina? Our testimony to our durability, forbearance, and true value?

"For I know the plans I have for you," declares the Lord, "plans to prosper you and not to harm you, plans to give you hope and a future" (Jeremiah 29:11, NIV).

Approach Vectors

If you habitually think less of yourself then, without even trying, you initiate a self-fulfilling prophecy. At some point, you have to acquire a credible standard of reference to gauge who you believe yourself to be. At a minimum, this should allow you to begin the process of identifying and ultimately appreciating your inalienable value.

A few years ago, according to the societal predisposition of my awesome country Canada, I was classified as a Senior. Now, not everyone defines the requirements for this auspicious life stage in the same manner. Some federal, provincial, and private entities bestow the title on those who have attained the silver-lined age of fifty-five. (That was me back then by the way). Others require an individual to be sixty or sixty-five years old. That then gave me a minimum of five to ten years to potentially nurture my denial. I figure if it took that long to wrestle with the reality of turning fifty-five, then by the time I am actually permitted to graciously scale the misty heights of my sixth decade, all arguments to the contrary will be null and void.

As I face this stage of my life, my understanding on what has transpired thus far to get me to this point has taken a quantifiable turn. I presume the older one gets, the more one takes stock of one's life. It's natural to weigh what you thought of, desired, or planned for your life as a young man with where you stand now, especially if you find yourself on the other end of the spectrum today. Borrowing an analogy from the golfing world, I have been giving much thought on the so-called *sweet spot* of my life of late.

In simple terms, a sweet spot is a place where a combination of factors results in a maximum response for a given amount of effort. Now, given my gender (male), and statistically speaking, I am naturally inclined to rate myself through performance or accomplishments. While these are not only characteristic of men, they are not inherently bad indicators of a person's worth. However, they are certainly not the healthiest ways to gauge one's equilibrium and value. Our society intensively promotes the successful, the strong, the popular, the beautiful—again, traits and positions that are not in themselves wrong. But when you are forced to measure yourself against such demanding, or in some cases, unforgiving standards and find yourself unable to live up to them, then your inner man, your psyche, your spirit, becomes weighted down and diminished. At times, it has been challenging to identify if I even have a sweet spot, in contrast to actually living out of one. To that end, I figured, why not work with what I know:

> • *I am a husband of more than thirty-three years to a woman who I am learning daily has more value and love to offer than I have sufficiently acknowledged.*

- *I am a father of the most awesome adult children a man could ask for.*

- *I have now transcended from Fatherhood to Grandparent with the arrival of my three Grandsons.*

- *I've had the opportunity to taste the sweetness of a dream fulfilled through the privilege of piloting aircraft in Northern Ireland in the United Kingdom; over the prairies of Alberta and in the mountains of British Columbia in Canada; and the Northwestern States of the USA.*

- *I have been blessed with a rich ancestral heritage that spans not only generations but continents, countries, and islands around the world.*

- *I believe in a Creator who unconditionally accepts me as I am, flaws and all, but loves me enough to elevate me to a position of sonship.*

These are just a few things that help me answer significant questions on my part. I still fail and make mistakes at times, but I am reminded that growing older and having your once black follicles turn grey (those that remain anyway) are more badges of honour[i] than a banner stigmatizing who you are as a person. After all, as stated before, wisdom and knowledge come through experience. Experience takes time and effort, and yes, even self-doubt and failure are valuable commodities, indispensable to the repository of knowledge one gains in a lifetime.

If left unchecked, our thought processes can and, in many cases, will define how we view ourselves. They also filter our perceptions on how (we think) others see us. So, how does one acquire a balanced, healthy thought life that provides for an honest perspective of oneself? For starters, we have to demystify and deconstruct some incorrect belief systems. Something that I am sure most of us wrestle with is our inability to properly steward our thought life. You cannot have a life apart from how you think. There are no parallel universes wherein we exist on one mental plane while coexisting separately in another. The influences we generate or respond to in our immediate surroundings showcase who we are and how we function.

If you habitually think less of yourself, then, without even trying, you initiate a self-fulfilling prophecy. At some point, one requires access to a definitive and credible standard of reference that can be used to gauge who you believe yourself to be. At a minimum, this should allow you to begin the process of identifying and ultimately, appreciating your distinctive value. Quantifying our self-worth based upon our own error-prone, man-made assumptions and life experiences is the epitome of self-delusion and usually leads to self-reproach, which, as we all (should) know, does not exactly lend itself to the edification of the inner man. As you get to know me, even peripherally, you will be afforded a glimpse into how I think, though not necessarily what my thoughts are.

Sixty-one years ago, I entered this physical plane. For as long as I can remember, over the intervening years any exposure to unexpected and significantly unpleasant events, would always affect me on a deep, personal level. I would always find myself taking stock of the immediate present. Dislocating oneself from the past, in order to function and remain acclimatized to the here and now, can be a challenge to one's mental equilibrium—especially if the experiences have been in any way, shape, or form traumatic. Please understand, I am not recommending we arbitrarily dispose of past experiences, whether they have been less than pleasant or full of contentment. In our zeal to stop any current imbalance in our lives, let's not ignore life lessons from the past, which allow us to glean valuable insight for our present and future selves.

I have come to realize this is not just about my desire to reminisce, but more about catching sight of the vistas breaking for the future. These cannot come into view without having an understanding of the value of where you have come from, or the things you have experienced.

So, why does it take us so long to see and grasp what is important in life? There are times in our lives when we undergo super-heated processes which allow for the separation and extraction of what is pure and valuable. Yes, including those things we would rather do without, like sorrow, financial destitution, hurtful relationships, or questionable health. These and other elements in life somehow add to those areas of our inner selves by way of the refining process. This then showcases our true natures—our spirits. These are of more value than any weight in gold.

If I had the knowledge and wisdom I have today, back when I was mediating arguments between what my then nineteen-year-old, testosterone-charged mind thought was right, versus what was truth, I might have gained insight earlier. But I am encouraged nonetheless. Even Moses, yes, the same one of Old Testament Egypt, needed eighty years to prep for a calling, which for all intents and purposes seemed like it was geared for a younger man's portfolio. Compared to him, I am now in my adolescent early sixties. This gives me reason to hope, as I have so much yet to learn.

> *Finally, brothers and sisters, whatever is true, whatever is noble, whatever is right, whatever is pure, whatever is lovely, whatever is admirable—if anything is excellent or praiseworthy—think about such things (Philippians 4:8, NIV).*

Landing Checklist

Courage always looks for the faint of heart because they are fertile ground, waiting to be watered into hope. It's also Courage's nature to use the very things which would intimidate or keep us fearful, by extracting and refining them into that which reveals and adds to our true mettle and value.

No matter the stage of life you currently find yourself in, certain experiences will have imprinted themselves on you in one form or another. Some have been helpful and hopeful, others less so. Some may have already reached an ending, but not every journey comes to a definable or acceptable conclusion. As much as we would like to have the stories of our lives resolved and neatly packaged, some aspects of our narratives remain without closure. Even so, we are not excluded from having a full, productive, and enjoyable life. We all endeavour to see our dreams come to fruition, even when life's tensions burden us.

So, let's say you awaken to a new day, like you have done a thousand times before. You sit up and reflect on your previous night's sleep. There is a lingering desire to crawl back under the sheets, as they represent a safe place, because when you are asleep, the problems and pressures you struggle through in your day-to-day life are temporarily held at bay. Those same pressures seem to have an excellent on-time arrival record whenever your eyes open from a night's slumber.

Now awake, you are faced with a choice. Do you shrink back from the looming, dark rain clouds in your mind, which were waiting in ambush to cause another day of mental struggle? Or do you stare them down until they release their moisture unto the parched ground of your worry, regret, or disillusionment?

I believe Courage always looks for the faint of heart, because they are fertile ground, waiting to be watered into hope. It's also Courage's nature to use the very things which would intimidate or keep us fearful, by extracting and refining them into that which reveals and adds to our true mettle and value.

So, with all of that in mind, how do you see yourself? Or a better question may be, how *can* you see yourself? How can you truly determine who you are and identify your value? We, of course, can look in a mirror and see our reflection. Our visual receptors receive and transfer the image via our optic nerve to our brain. These images somehow become filtered and interpreted through our preconceptions, which invariably distort our view and target us with toxic accusations such as:

- You are too fat
- You are too short
- You are a loser
- You will never amount to anything
- You are not attractive

- You will never be loved or find love
- You are useless
- You will never get it right
- You are hopeless

When sound waves propagate, they either bounce off, get diffused by, or get absorbed into a given surface or object. So too can our perceptions. They can form deep-rooted impressions in our minds, not all of them healthy. Just as sound waves under normal circumstances are invisible, they still have great impact, especially if the decibel level climbs beyond what is safe. Over time, our senses become attuned to our environment, just as a physically blind person tends to have more acute hearing than someone with normal vision. Interestingly, there is an unrealized irony when considering those who have fully functioning vision; they at times may find themselves without (in)sight when attempting to see things clearly.

Every day, our thoughts are inundated with a torrent of uninvited and unfiltered information. Whether we receive this from the voice inside our head or from an external source, we automatically assimilate this data. If our self-esteem is not a balanced or healthy one, you risk processing this information in a degenerative fashion. After all, our inner critic tends to drown out the healthy, external voices that attempt to bring us healing, wholeness, and the right perspective. Therefore, our challenge lies in learning how to filter out the negative aspects of this data influx.

When you don't have a clear understanding or acceptance of your true value, it can be a difficult task to be objective about yourself. We tend to be more subjective, usually as a result of the impact of life's more painful experiences. This may cause us to view ourselves in the lowest common denominator. This in turn can form mental or emotional stresses, which may even contribute to unexpected physical conditions like high blood pressure.

Therefore, if our judgement about our true selves is constrained because of our preconceived notions, or external forces, we have to take some risks, some of which may fly in the face of the very things you believe, see, or feel are happening to you. To help us recognize if we are in the isolation chamber of self-recrimination, or shackled with self-doubt, taking formative steps, however risky, will allow us to see the deception behind our overburdened thought processes, and call them out for what they truly are—lies about our true worth.

Undertaking some of these risks may require a change of scenery (physical or emotional), or maybe even a change in relationships. Possibly, even a change in your value system exercised through faith in something, or someone greater than yourself. Half the battle of establishing a paradigm shift in your thinking involves recognizing the need for change in the first place. This recognition may come about through the assistance of friends, family, professionals, or even clergy. Regardless, even while wrestling with the dark filters through which you may be currently viewing things, there is hope for renewed clarity and vision for your life.

For myself, I do not claim to have attained perfection or acquired all the answers I've been seeking. As the years have unfolded since the early days of my childhood, I have discovered I not only miss the precious gift of childlike innocence, but the unforced expectations which go along with it as well. This realization has come to the forefront with poignant force as I pause to consider my current life with the eyes, ears, scars, and weariness of an adult. I do not mean to belittle the fact that life happens. Yes, as you get older, the once smooth, soft, and pliable elements of innocence (not to mention skin) inevitably become exposed to the harsh realities contained in the forces arrayed against it. Unfortunately, over time, this may lead to hardness and brittleness of the heart. But at this juncture in my life, you could say I have been on a Search and Rescue mission to recapture that which has eluded me over the years. While for the most part it has been a successful endeavour, the mission continues.

The irony in all this is that sometimes in order to regain a healthy and informed perspective, you have to retrace your steps through what could be construed as enemy territory—Sorrow, Loss, Regret, Pain...to name a few. The good news is that while it can be a painful and at times unpleasant process, it's attainable. It also helps to not travel alone, especially when traversing such familiar valleys of darkness. It's always beneficial to partner with those willing to walk with you as you learn to once again experience life in all its fullness. I guess you could say it requires an intervention—one in which everyone may or may not share a similar experience. However, giving myself permission to hope, in spite of the current emotional scenery I happen to be travelling through, is more than worth the risk when taking such leaps of faith.

STAFFORD W. EDWARDS

We are hard pressed on every side, but not crushed; perplexed, but not in despair; persecuted, but not abandoned; struck down, but not destroyed (2 Corinthians 4:8-9, NIV).

Touchdown

At the time of this writing, it has been over two years since the start of the global COVID-19 pandemic—an unexpected scenario, which, on a global scale, has forced the entire planetary population to reassess and re-evaluate its priorities, not only health related, but personal, financial, and otherwise.

This season has caused many to look individually and collectively inward. For some, this introspection has revealed unexpected, and in some cases, unrecognizable things in themselves which were not readily evident prior to the pandemic. Some of these revelations have brought out the best in some and the worst in others. What this does not preclude however, is the option of making proper choices. For the most part we all have that opportunity; some would say obligation.

I have had the privilege of many departures and arrivals throughout life, and this stage of my journey is no different. As I navigate the current landscape, my perspective has not only been influenced by time and experience, but by intentionality; by the very choices I have made. Not all have been wise or well thought out, and some have been easier than others, but all have been part and parcel in defining who I am today.

Looking back over the years and recalling the various situations, circumstances, and scenarios I have faced, what has become more evident to me, is the evolution of my personality. Now entering my sixth decade, I find myself giving more thought to how I define myself, as opposed to how others define who I am. While the journey over the intervening years has, at times, proven challenging, there have also been many moments of exhilaration. I am looking forward to experiencing even more of what life has to offer with whatever time remains. Even so, I have learned that some aspects of lost opportunities and time can be redeemed. This has less to do with me or my abilities and more to do with whom I have placed my trust and faith in.

Within each of the preceding chapters, I have allocated at least one biblical scripture reference. They have been guideposts along my journey—mile markers highlighting moments of clarity or confusion, rest or restlessness, courage or fear, love or loneliness. For any quantifiable success or failure in life I have experienced, I have been wrapped with God's mercy and compassion. I may not have always felt that way during those moments, but that does not make it any less true.

I am not here to dictate to you a formula, methodology, or ideology for establishing a fulfilled life. I can only express to you, who has been my redeeming source when I felt helpless, weak, or lost. I have to give all credit and honour to the One who has strengthened and lifted me up—Jesus Christ. I have discovered that, apart from Him, I can do nothing. No amount of positive thinking, tradition, or religious practice will aid me in being who I was created to be. In Jesus I have a friend and confidant, someone who unconditionally accepts me as I am—flaws and all, without any judgement. It's refreshing and liberating to know you are accepted as is, without conditions. I am allowed to grow and evolve in my humanity, knowing I am seen and loved in spite of any real or perceived shortcomings. That is why my trust in Jesus is without reservation. I am who I am because of Him.

I am also glad I have been given a sound mind, one that is capable of reason. When we are faced with situations or circumstances that challenge our perceptions or cause us to question what is true or false, even then we are free to decide for ourselves and be who we wish to be without fear of sanction by God. He never forces Himself on you. He is that loving and full of Grace.

So, as I mentioned at the beginning, my sincerest hope for you through this book is one of encouragement, no matter how disconnected, disillusioned, or disenfranchised you may be feeling. If I have provided even a small intersection of renewed hope along your own life journey, then my efforts have been fully rewarded.

May God Bless You.

Come to me, all you who are weary and burdened, and I will give you rest. Take my yoke upon you and learn from me, for I am gentle and humble in heart, and you will find rest for your souls. For my yoke is easy and my burden is light (Matthew 11:28-30, NIV).

Acknowledgements

This literary journey would not have been made possible without the love, encouragement, wisdom, and expertise of some very special people, who saw in me gifts which I either did not recognize or was initially too afraid to develop.

To my extraordinary wife of over thirty-three years, I cannot thank God enough for who I have become because of your love and patience. Truly, I am a better man because of you.

To my children, including Isaac, who we will laugh with again one day: *"Like arrows in the hands of a warrior are children born in one's youth. Blessed is the man whose quiver is full of them"* (Psalm 127:4-5, NIV). Each of you, through your individual personality and expression of love, continually gift me with joy, purpose, and uncountable blessings.

To Mom and Dad: Not only am I indebted to you for my existence, I am also humbled, honoured, and immeasurably grateful to be called your son. Thank you for the love you have demonstrated and lessons you taught me over the years which have allowed me to gain wisdom.

To my good friend (and unexpected mentor), retired Ottawa Police Superintendent, Isobel Granger, of the Ottawa Police Service. If not for your divinely appointed invitation to attend a writing conference with you five years ago, I would never have embarked on this adventure. Thank you so much for keeping me on track while on this literary journey, especially when the way forward seemed obscured.

To my editor, Elizabeth Boden. From your first review of my manuscript, you immediately elevated and refined what I was trying to say. You have a gift that translates raw material into a level of refinement that is astounding. Thank you so much for your incisive and insightful recommendations.

I would also like to acknowledge those who took time out of their busy lives to beta read my manuscript; I cannot thank you enough for your feedback. It was immeasurably beneficial.

And most importantly, I would like to thank You, God, for, well...everything! Without You none of this would have even been possible. My life, my family, my friends, and my associates are treasures received from You that I can never fully repay. I will also continue to exercise and steward the gifts and talents You have graced me with.

Glossary

APPROACH VECTOR—The vector or approved deviation for an assigned arrival procedure which may contain altitude or speed restrictions

ATC—Air Traffic Control

CONTRAILS—Condensation Trails—streaks of condensed water vapour created by aircraft flying at high altitudes

GPA—Grade Point Average

HYPOXIA—A condition in which the body, or a specific region (e.g., the brain) is deprived of adequate oxygen supply.

SEAL Team—The United States Navy, Sea, Air, and Land (SEAL) specialized military team

TRANSITION ALTITUDE—a published height above sea level at which pilots, climbing to their cruising level, change their barometric altimeter setting from the local regional pressure setting to the common international standard setting of 1013.2hPa.

---

[i] *The glory of young men is their strength, and the splendour of old men is their grey head (Proverbs 20:29, NKJV).*

Don't miss out!

Visit the website below and you can sign up to receive emails whenever Stafford W. Edwards publishes a new book. There's no charge and no obligation.

https://books2read.com/r/B-A-TLIV-JCXBC

BOOKS2READ

Connecting independent readers to independent writers.

About the Author

I hail from the small Caribbean island of Jamaica in the West Indies. I emigrated with my parents and younger brother to Alberta Canada at the age of seventeen, over forty-four years ago.

After graduating from high school in Edmonton, I attended the Southern Alberta Institute of Technology in Calgary, where I acquired my Aircraft Maintenance Engineering Diploma. Shortly thereafter, I applied to Trinity Western University in Langley, British Columbia, where I completed my Aviation Technology Degree and received my Commercial Pilot's license, Multi-Engine Instrument Rating, and Float Plane Endorsements.

My initial career started with the Federal Government of Canada, in Transport Canada's Air Traffic Control System. My first posting was as an Air Traffic Control Flight Planner in the control tower of a small regional air-port—Toronto's Buttonville Airport (CYKZ) in Markham, Ontario. After a few years, I transferred to Canada's busiest airport, Lester B. Pearson International (CYYZ) in Toronto, where I worked in the control tower before transitioning to the Toronto Area Control (Radar) Centre. Thereafter, my career path diverted into Information Technology, a vocation in which I still continue to this day.

Read more at https://contrails.ca.

www.ingramcontent.com/pod-product-compliance
Lightning Source LLC
Chambersburg PA
CBHW021334060726
47591CB00006B/2020